Shaken
and
Moved

Shaken
and
Moved

MARK RASQUINHA

PARTRIDGE

To order additional copies of this book, contact
Partridge India
000 800 10062 62
orders.india@partridgepublishing.com

www.partridgepublishing.com/india

Contents

CHAPTER 1

A Troubled Past

As human beings we are obsessed with reason, and as soon as a phenomenon occurs, we are intrigued to make sense of it. While each of us relies on our own varied experiences to make sense of what has happened, we also invariably find the need to dismiss other reasons.

On the 25 April 2015, an earthquake of magnitude 7.8 rocked the Himalayan country of Nepal. As reports emerged of how the world's tallest peak Mount Everest had gotten shorter, people began to joke about how people who had scaled the peak earlier would have climbed higher than the ones who would make attempts in the future. There was misery at the base camp of Mount Everest. The earthquake, which is now popularly known to many as the Gorkha earthquake, had been a sever shake after a long period of eighty years. 'Every 80 years we have a severe earthquake and then we rebuild,' these were the words of many individuals that I came across on the streets of Kathmandu, the capital city of Nepal.

According to most sources in the media, the earthquake occurred at 11.56 Nepal Standard Time (NST). The result was death and destruction, while the death toll is put at over 8,000 people, the number of injured folk hovered around

19,000. The epicentre of the quake was a village named Barpak, situated in the Gorkha district. The hypocentre which is the depth of the quake was an estimated fifteen kilometres.

Nepal has a history of earth quakes, the last one with such a magnitude occurred in the year 1934. It was called the Nepal–Bihar Earthquake. The 8.0 magnitude earthquake affected several parts of India. The parts of Nepal that suffered the most were the Kathmandu Valley, Bhaktapur, and Patan. Given the period of time, it is not surprising that almost all buildings had collapsed. It is reported that not a single building could be found standing in the village of Sitamarhi. The story was similar in almost all parts of the country. But, as the mud settled, Nepal began to put the pieces in place and moved on.

In the modern context, any story surrounding a disaster will have two sides to it. The first is what happens in the cities and the other is what happens in the villages. Often importance is given to matters pertaining to the city, where death and destruction is less severe. The other and more important side is the story of the rural conditions which are either ignored or they rely on the stories told on the cities. Experiencing the taste of death is not something that is different depending on the location of death and destruction. The agony and sorrow of losing a loved one, the uncertainty of the future left the people of Nepal bitter.

The Earthquake had managed to trigger an avalanche which, Nepali media reported, killed around nineteen people. There were further avalanches that were triggered as a result of the aftershocks which left several people missing. What followed this earthquake was the displacement of hundreds of thousands of people from their homes. Not only were the homes of people but even the world heritage site in Kathmandu were destroyed. The irony is that experts and researchers had predicted that the earthquake in Nepal was long overdue. Of course they could not predict when exactly it was going to take place, but they had read the signs. Despite the warnings, houses were not evacuated, there was no suitable disaster management plan put in place. If the young Government of Nepal had perhaps taken thing more seriously, may be the number of deaths could have been reduced. It is true that there will always be ifs and buts in an event of a disaster. Yet, it is these Ifs and buts that help us ask the question. What is the use of all the researches that we conduct as researchers? What is the point of research if it is not applicable to society and the people studied in the research? It would be inappropriate for me to be so hard on the researcher's studying the movement of the plates under us all. May be I am overwhelmed by the grief I witnessed in Nepal, but my question reiterates the fact that that there is no formidable system put in place that helps research be applicable to the ground.

To say that scientists did not try to warn the government about what was to come would be inaccurate. Nepal has been an area of study for many years, since it sits on the peripherals of the Indo-Australian plate, which is pushing itself under the Eurasian plate. It is the coming together of these two plates that has given rise to the Himalayan Mountain range. According to *Nature*, a popular online magazine, the Indo-Australian plate is believed to be pushing itself under the Eurasian plate at a rate of around two inches per year. Geologically speaking, that is very fast according to Lung S. Chan, a geophysicist at the University of Hong Kong.

Another scientist who perhaps had a lot more to say about the earthquake was Laurent Bollinger of the CEA research agency in France. In his study, a team of scientists had dug trenches along the fault line. With the help of carbon dating on charcoal, they found that certain segments of rock had not moved for nearly 700 years. This reading was accurate with what the people of Nepal had to say. 'Every eighty years, there will be a big Earthquake', almost like every generation of the Nepali people were destined to witness a tragedy such as this.

Bollinger's team had warned the Nepal Geological Society meeting in early April that the same patter could occur again. The warning are still plenty and what is being done can still be questioned; by the time you are reading this book it may be too late or you may hear of another earthquake. As Bollinger points out, the last earthquake may not have been enough to relieve all the pressure that exists between the rocks.

The calculations by scientists suggest that the previous two earthquakes of magnitude 7.8 and 7.4 were probably not big enough to rupture all the way to the surface, so there is likely to be more strain stored; there could hence be another earthquake in the coming decades.

What that means for people like me who have been on the ground is heartbreaking. What it does is – it tests away hope. This book is the result of hope that I carried with me into Nepal. The belief that I could do something and bring about a smile on the face of people I hadn't seen before. At times, if you begin to feel like I did something good, correct yourself that very instance, for I am the messenger who is telling the story. There has much greater suffering the ground has witnessed. This is my attempt to tell their story.

CHAPTER 2

The Earth Shook

This was the first wedding in the house of Nar Bhadur Nepali. It was also the wedding of his only daughter, Saritha. It was a time of mixed emotions for him; on one hand, he felt he was on the verge of completing his primary responsibilities as a father and, on the other hand, his only daughter, who he was very fond of, would leave him to begin a life with her new found companion. A mirage of thoughts flowed through Nar's mind; Marriages are complex. Having been married for almost twenty years, he had plenty of experience.

What struck me the most in my conversation with Nar was his forward views on marriage as an institution, 'Marriage is easy for a boy; other than the addition of another human relation around you, everything else remains the same. Life for a girl is different, as soon as she is married, everything around her will change'. Saritha would have to move to a new village that was at least a day-and-a-half travel from her paternal home. This was a big step for her, and even if she did not realise it, her father was aware of the twists and turns that were coming up in her life.

Nevertheless, to organise a wedding in his household was an accomplishment for Nar Bhadur. The courtyards were abuzz with little children playing their games. The sun was out in all its glory, and in its glittering light, the vestments of the village folk painted a picture of grandeur. It was the wedding ceremony of Nar's only daughter. A busy morning greeted the wedding day, 'We were running late, despite preparing for months. It felt like nothing was going to plan'. It was a good thing that the sun goes up by 4.15 a.m. in this part of the world. It gives people here so much more time during the day.

Had he known there were greater convolutions coming up in his life, Nar would have chosen another day to bid his young daughter a new life. 'That is the nature of natural calamities, only God has control on them. We can only pray to him and ask for his protection, yet at times our prayers can fall on deaf ears'. There is a lot of disappointment visible on Nar's face as he recalls the event of 25 April 2015. There were doubts if we could start the wedding on time, most of our family and friends had travelled great distances to grace the occasion. Nar points to a cousin of his sitting across the road and says he has to walk several miles before he can get to a road and once on the local bus it is a six-hour journey to get here. They were all here well in advance. Somehow by the grace of God, we were able to start on time. It was also the grace of God that we were having the ceremony out in the open. Most of our family, friends, and neighbours were out with us.

There was no problem during the ceremony; all was calm. 'The only sounds we could hear was the sound of happiness, fun, and laughter. All of a sudden, some of us felt mild shakes in the ground, nothing we had not seen or felt before, but then there was a large 'thud', if any part of your body was connected to the ground you could have felt it'. In the distance, the hills were falling apart. A landslide on not just one hill, but almost every hill in the range surrounding. In every direction, people were scrambling, screaming 'Bhookump! Bhookump aya!'. Disaster had struck us out of nowhere. Most people were already terrified by the movement of the ground as it got really violent. Even though it lasted only for a short while, the manner in which it shook made each and every one cry out for mercy. At times we feel powerful, but in moments like that you are reminded of the fact that 'we are such small creatures living in this serenity'. We are so sure that we will see the next day and all the other days that will follow up until we get old. The truth is very different in reality. 'The truth is we are like that young bird on the grass, fairly confident of it surrounding and inherent assurance that life will continue in the manner in which it has for all this while. The bird is unaware of the vulture's presence and its life is always at risk'.

Everybody says we are lucky, and the wedding saved most of us. Had it not been for the ceremony some of the folk would have been indoors. A good number of people would have lost their lives, all close and dear ones.

'I believe it would have been better if we lost our lives'. Once the disaster struck, how was Nar supposed to let his daughter go with a family that was unsure about having a house to stay in? The ceremony was done and with it went his ability to make any decisions on behalf of his daughter. Her in-laws decided they would leave with her, even if it meant cutting short the celebrations. Nar's quiet objections did not affect their decision, and he was forced to toe the line. 'Making an argument at a time like that is not proper; we have to be supportive of each other. Furthermore my house had fallen flat on to the ground. The aluminium sheet for makeshift shelters is not enough to house so many people'.

The wedding party left as soon as they could with Saritha, and for the next three days, there would be no news from her. Nar had little time to ponder her situation as he worked to desperately salvage what little wood remained of his house. His initial efforts yielded a little furniture and some clothes. The more pressing issue were bodies in the neighbourhood that needed to be buried. The dilemma was what could he tend to first? Was it more important to look at his own house or was it more important to look at pressing matters of the community. 'Some of our neighbours were injured and needed care. We had to help them salvage what they could from their houses'.

The biggest task for each individual was to secure food and shelter. The community waited for relief materials to come. Some of the neighbouring villages received aid, but nothing came to Nar Bhadure Nepali's village. It has been seven days since the earthquake struck. The village community finally received some amount of aid in the form of three kilograms of rice, dahl, and a packet of cooking oil for each member of family.

CHAPTER 3

Indian Media, Go Home

There is a very big reason as to why I chose to be an academic rather than a journalist. In my limited experience, I had already figured that journalism was sold. I did get exposed to most of the practices of journalists. I did share these experiences with all the senior journalists I knew. My interactions only helped me confirm the fact that journalism was no longer about bringing truth to light. Is there any hope to salvage the sorry state is a debate that is not the purpose of the book. Yet, there is a reason as to why 'Indian Media, Go Home' has found a chapter in this book. It is true that I am a lecturer of journalism; it is also true that I have stopped reading most of the newspapers and watching most of our prime time 'infotainment shows'. The only time I do consume the above-mentioned forms of media is when I have to prepare for a class.

Now it had been a little more than a year since I began lecturing on issues related to the media. I spoke about various theories related to communication and the media in my class rooms. My journey to this point was not easy. Though being late at almost every stage of my academic life, I had in some sense figured out what I wanted to do and more importantly 'Why' I wanted to do it. I will say that my

journey to becoming a young lecturer was not easy because
every time I approached my seniors or mentors, I was advised
to first gain some experience in the field of journalism.
There were people who would even find me jobs in the local
papers. It wasn't that I had absolutely no experience being
a journalist. I had spent the last two years being a freelance
journalist writing for local newspapers. I had experienced
most of what a journalist of my age had experienced. The
only thing I missed out on was the experience of working
among journalists and working within the systems of the
corporate houses that run most of India's media.

Journalism for me as an academic is an idea. In its most
pure form, it stands for certain values without which society
would find it difficult to function. The power of journalism
has been universally understood by every strata of society.
Today, that field is complex. I could very well enter this
field with the idea of changing it. Would I survive it, is
again a matter of debate. In my reading of the situation, I
would by no means survive it simply because I would have
to compromise on my principals. I believe the failure to
understand that situation is corrupting journalism as an
education. As more and more people from the industry
come in to teach journalism, they fail to teach students that
journalism is an idea that stands for a few things. Instead
they teach students about journalism as a profession. The
larger problem here is education being tuned to the markets
and being made into an industry.

The twitter war that broke out with #Indianmediagohome
trending in Nepal is just a symptom of a disease that is
growing within media education. I was eager to verify some
of the reports that I believe were rashly sprayed across all
platforms related to the media in India. On my first day in

Nepal, I happened to meet several members of the Nepali–Tibetan community. Among them were two boys who had caught my attention, they did not like me too much; I could tell by the vibes I received all day. I tried my best to strike up a conversation with almost everybody around me. While most were cordial in their interactions, the two boys kept their distance. I wondered why at the time, but given the tasks at hand, I did not care too much.

As we passed the country side, the destruction caused by the earthquake in the rural areas came to the fore. In spite of the beauty that mesmerised us, the plight of the people we passed on our journey only saddened the soul. How could a place this beautiful be so harsh? The occasional glimpses of development work in the area hinted at answers that were best left without any discussion. The journey carrying relief material was by no means easy. At times the roads disappeared and at other times the truck did not have enough power to make the steep climb. Finishing the date on schedule seemed incomprehensible.

After a late supper, most of us began calling it a night. Some others decided to spend time creating happiness. There were the singing popular Bollywood songs. It was hard to understand where people got that kind of energy from. As the singing and the jokes continued into the night, I found myself in the company of these two boys. The topic of discussion was an interesting one 'Democracy Vs Monarchy'. The discussion did have a global flavour to it. We had a couple of Americans who to my surprise did not give democracy the respect that one would assume it would get from an American. Gregory was highly critical of democracy and looked at it as a system that had been manipulated and degraded by capitalism. As the discussion continued and my two friends realised I was not an 'Indian Journalist', they jumped to make conversation with me.

'Shit man! I thought you were an Indian Journalist and that's why I did not talk to you. I didn't even know why you were here'. I was taken aback by the hatred for the Indian journalist. As I began to dig deeper, I did not have much sympathy myself. As I laboured to understand this new found hatred for the Indian journalist, I explained to them that I taught journalism and my visit was an attempt to ensure future journalists did not hurt the people they serve. I could tell I had touched a sensitive chord. Tashi my friend went on to narrate a story that would make me shameful. 'Once the earthquake hit us, there was so much of grief and panic around. The journalists did not make life easy as we tried to help people. I was asked by the journalist if I was thankful to India for all the aid?' He pointed out to the aid we were carrying and told me that the money for the aid was raised by the Tibetan community of Nepal and all the money was raised from within. 'We have not asked anybody from outside for anything'.

India had provided some relief material, but was it right to demand a thank you note from Nepal or its people. The question we must ask ourselves is, 'Was there a need to play politics?' The fact that politics was at play was evident by the kind of coverage we were witnessing. Most stories were not about the people but what the Indian community or Indian defence personnel were doing to help. At times journalist went up to people and asked them how they felt about losing a loved one, immediately after people had suffered such grievous losses. In times like this, it helps to be a little sensitive to the suffering of people.

The Indian media failed not only its people but the Indian Democracy. It has been a month since #Indianmediagohome made headlines. There have been few articles in the mainstream media that have critically evaluated the role of the Indian media in Nepal. Ten days after the 7.8 earthquake had hit Nepal, the presence of India in Nepal was close to nil. The watchdog should have sniffed out a failure of diplomatic relations. Yet, no stories made headlines criticising the government. There should have been follow-up stories on the presence and influence China was wielding in Nepal. If this had happened, the Indian government would have faced pressure and done something to improve ties with Nepal.

I could feel the sadness in the voices of my Nepali friends as they all fell asleep. I sat up for a while with Gregory and Bryan who were journalism students back in the United States of America. We discussed how the local media had failed to report about the villages we were visiting. The local representative did mention how one journalist from Nepal said he would mention the name of all villages in Lalithpur and had failed to do so. The result was another three days of no relief. The media is extremely important but what was happening with the media in Nepal only made people hate it. I wondered if that could happen in India. Could we grow tired of questioning our media or are we too disillusioned already? My thoughts were interrupted as the Earth began to move, again!

CHAPTER 4

A Helping Hand

This chapter may not be as elaborate as the others. Yet it is one of the most important chapters. If this phase had not passed I would have never had the courage to go to Nepal. It had been a week since the earthquake had rocked the Kathmandu valley and its surroundings. The pictures of death and destruction had caused me some sleepless nights. I did not know what to do or how I could help. Of course, I could help with a monetary donation to the people in distress; there were a good number of people who were already doing it. Somehow I could not subscribe to just making a contribution and being done with it.

As mentioned earlier, I am a young academic with an avant-garde approach to education. 'Education must be applied to society, if not, there is no use to education', says Rev Fr Ambrose Pinto SJ. I have been associated with him for a good seven years now. He was my principal back been my mentor. During my many visits to his office, I would discuss academics and social issues. During one of my visits, he told me about his early days as a lecturer. 'Visit places that have witnessed conflict, death, and destruction. Understand the struggles of people, only then education becomes meaningful', he said. During the course of that conversation, Fr Ambrose went on to narrate examples of how he had visited areas that had witnessed riots to understand the different caste politics that shape up after any communal destructions. I felt uncomfortable as I had realised the only way I could become relevant in a classroom was by gaining these experiences and presenting them to the class.

The desire to go to Nepal was there, but the lack of experience showed; fear was another factor. In the twenty-eight years of my life, I had not crossed the peripherals of Maharashtra in western India. The idea that I could go as a volunteer did not occur to me. It was one evening as I went through the daily news feeds on my Facebook wall that I came across a post from one of my friends. It was about an American, Paul Baroud, and his efforts as a volunteer. He had put up a picture of himself leaving the United States for Nepal. He had also asked people to pledge an amount that he could use to do relief work. That picture showed me the path I should take. I was quick to get in touch with him, although I could not pledge an amount. Paul told me there were plenty of organisations working in Nepal, and I could join any of them.

Culturally, India is very different from most other countries, and I was an introvert in many ways. I was scared of getting into the unknown. I did not know about airport procedures, and frankly getting through each small step required every ounce of concentration I could muster. Yes, it was scary! At the offset, my efforts to get in touch with reputed relief organisations were yielding no results. I got in touch with a Tibetan activist, named Tenzing Tsundue, a friend who I met when he was a speaker at one of the guest lecture sessions in my postgraduate programme. He was kind enough to share a few contacts; I tried contacting Passang, the President of the Regional Tibetan Youth Congress. It wasn't easy as in the lead up to my departure from Bangalore. Passang was busy conducting relief operations in the remotest possible parts of Nepal. His phone was never in coverage area and that scared me even more.

If you are a young student reading this book, there is an important lesson to be learnt. It does not matter if you study in Oxford, London or Oxford, Bangalore, if you cannot network with people around you. Tenzing spoke to thirty students in my class. I can assure you that not more than two to five people in that class are still in touch with him. There is a question you must ask yourself now. How many guest lecturers or different people who have come to speak to you in college are you in touch with? If the answer to that question is disappointing, it is time to pull your socks up because college is all about putting you in touch with people from different disciplines and their work that may help give you a toehold in your future ventures.

My journey to Nepal was long, even if my total travel time was a little more than three hours. That is something that surprised me about air travel. It takes you more time to get through the formalities, and the actual travel time is so short. Reflective of the situation at Kathmandu, I spent an entire day waiting to board a flight. Not that I am complaining; everything is fascinating to a first-time flyer, even getting through the winding lines and security. At Delhi, I saw the relief planes that were headed to Nepal. In my conversation with vendors who sold overpriced sandwiches at the airport, I learnt that the planes were stranded in Delhi for a long time. I was also informed that there was a problem between the Governments of India and Nepal. Although there were some reports in the media, there was nothing elaborate about what was going on between the governments. May be it was too soon for the media to get a hold of something, and in time, the real nature of diplomatic relations between these two neighbours will make its way to print.

Once I had reached Kathmandu, I did not find it difficult; Passang was the most reliable person I had met in a very long time. I was given the choice of staying in a hotel or staying with him. I felt there was a lot I could learn by staying with Passang, who even in the most difficult circumstances provided me with the warmest accommodations. It was late, yet he spent time talking to me about different things. We discussed everything from movies to politics before we called it a night. I was given a good picture of the relief work carried out by the RTYC. Armed now with a vague picture of what awaited me, and I dozed away one of the most peaceful nights I spent in Kathmandu.

CHAPTER 5

The Tibetans

The choice of freedom for an individual or a country is not about breaking chains that bind them. It is the choice that decides the manner in which one must live, so that he may enhance age-old values of respect, tolerance, and justice not so much for himself but others. The idea of freedom in the words of Ronald Reagan somehow captures the essence of the Tibetan freedom struggle. 'Freedom is never more than one generation away from extinction. We didn't pass it on to our children in the bloodstream. It must be fought for, protected, and handed on for them to do the same'. One senses the longing of every Tibetan to go back to their land within a few minutes of meeting them.

I came across the Tibetan folk on the first day on my Nepal mission. I had worked with the Tibetan community earlier in my college days. Never was I, the kind to join an organisation. This is simply because I saw myself as a critical thinker who was called to fight on the side of the marginalised. Nevertheless, this was the farthest I had travelled in my life and being with the Tibetan community provided me with a feeling of comfort and safety. During my college days, I had friends in the Tibetan student community, but my interactions with their elders and family were very limited. This would be the first time I would get to see at first-hand, a full-fledged Tibetan community.

Arriving from Bangalore, Passang and I would begin our journey from Kathmandu, the capital city and nerve centre of all relief efforts, I would first travel the Tibetan centre at

Boudha, Kathmandu. On the road, I witnessed the damage caused by the earthquake. It wasn't as bad as I had expected it to be. Most roads had the occasional building that had fallen down or one building that was on its way down. It certainly did not look as bad as the newspapers in India made it to be. I told Passang about my initial feelings of the place; I gave him a description of what the media had broadcasted to a million viewers back home. He informed me that this was the eastern side of Kathmandu which was not that badly affected by the earthquake. We continued with our journey, and in close to thirty minutes, we reached Boudha gate, which is one of Kathmandu's famous commercial centres. The Buddhist community centre was located in one of the narrowest of turnings. A majestic building stood in the midst of other houses decorated with flags. People around were dressed in traditional Tibetan attire. The architecture of the area was also traditionally Tibetan. The area I found myself in was home to the traditional Tibetan community of Nepal.

As soon as we got off the bike, Passang went on to enquire about the whereabouts of his mates. It seemed we were early, and he offered to show me around. It wasn't a palatial building but it was adequate. There was a ground floor that had two very big rooms; one was a large prayer hall while the other was a large dining hall. The ground floor had a big kitchen which was not attached to the main building. After a while, we were joined by the core committee of the RTYC. The previous day had been a hard day for the group. I was introduced to Yeshi and Tashi. Cordial as they were, these people did not come across like the Tibetans, I had met in Bangalore. In fact, they were a stark contrast.

In Bangalore, there are certain traits that you will notice among Tibetan students; of course, there will always be exceptions. However, most Tibetan students in Bangalore are introverts; very rarely will you find a Tibetan student that can hold her/his own in group discussions. There could be several factors that constitute reasons for the same. The difference could very well be between being at home and being far away from home. Yeshi was a strong, lion-hearted girl; at times she provided direction to the group. Tashi was incredible when it came to executing work that needed to be done, and as for my friend Passang, there were very strong ideologies and beliefs that I may not always agree with. What set him apart from his group was the hallmarks of a great leader. He was patient and listened to the views of his fellow companions. When he sat down to work, he made sure there were no lines that divided his team. Most importantly, he kept the greed of power in control, which let everyone interested in the project and own the group. Some of the discussions, in between the members of the group were remarkable. It was hard for me to be party to the group's decision-making process. It was not that they were discussing things I had not come across before. I did have suggestions, and I found it hard to keep opinions to myself and let them plan what they were going to do. I had to remind myself that I was there as an observer seeking to learn and help with whatever relief work that was entrusted to me.

Only a few minutes after I was introduced to the group, I witnessed the first discussion of the core group. The volunteers had returned from a rather difficult assignment the previous night. They were expected to distribute relief packages, which constituted of rice, dhal, and cooking oil to a place that was quite well-connected to the main city. While Passang and Tashi seemed to agree, Yeshi had other ideas. It was her convictions that were so inspiring for someone like me who had always run away from hard labour. 'What is the use of going to some place that already has received relief when there are other places that have not received any kind of aid?' she argued. This was supported by strong reasoning, and the others relented.

As the group split to find out which places could be covered, I got talking with Yeshi who helped me understand the problems local groups such as the RTYC was facing. The biggest problem she said was finding a place. 'There is lack of information right now; nobody knows what relief has reached where'. The group relied on personal contacts sitting within the administration of Nepal or a Facebook page titled 'Nepal 2015 Earthquake rescue'. This page was highly instrumental in helping local groups like the RTYC get in touch with local village representatives and co-ordinate the relief process.

Malta is a place in the remote areas of Lalithpur, and Yeshi was headed there. As the group scattered to more urgent pressing matters, I was left in the company of a young Tibetan girl, Negora Tenzing. She was well-spoken and worked as a receptionist in a nearby Tibetan hotel. Negora was going to teach me a lot about Tibetan culture in the next twenty-four hours.

As I mentioned earlier, the ground floor of the Tibetan centre had two major halls, one was for prayer and the other was the dining hall where I spent a good amount of time. At times the dining hall went silent, because there were no people in it and I would hear the sound of prayer. My curiosity prompted me to ask Negora what was the chanting about. She told me that every time there was a natural disaster like this, all the elders gathered and prayed for the people affected by the calamity. 'Today they are praying for the victims of the earthquake', she said. 'Why don't you join them in prayers?' I asked. She smiled at me and said 'we do the work'.

I was fascinated with the culture I had experienced. There was work combined with prayer which gave meaning to spirituality. Before I left Bangalore, I was bombarded with news of churches and people saying they were praying for the people of Nepal. I did not understand at the time why everybody only attended service, offered money, and washed their hands of it. Again I am sure there are exceptions but otherwise none of them even bothered finding out what kind of help was needed. None of us stopped to wonder if we could join the people of Nepal in prayer.

While I continued to ask questions and Negora continued to patiently put up with me, the rest of the volunteers had arrived. Work was about to begin. I was introduced to Gregory who was from the United States of America and was one of the volunteers working with the Tibetans. The task at hand was to first unload the relief material that had arrived. There was no discrimination in the manner in which we worked; both girls and boys carried the material. Once that was done, individual packets had to be made. Each rice bag contained three-and-a half kilograms of rice along with dhal and cooking oil. All volunteers split the work equally, everyone took turns. I would first use a bucket to put rice in a bag, another volunteer would hold the bag for me, after which the bag would go to another volunteer who's task was to tie the bag. Each of us kept shifting roles, at times I would tie the bag, and when I got bored of it, I would hold the bag for the rice to be put in. This removed monotony of work. Once all the bags were packed, the count began; there had to be relief for more than 250 families. Getting the estimated size of population requiring relief was the key. The group had witnessed instances of violence in the past when the relief material was insufficient and rioting began. Also we now knew we were going into areas that had not seen relief for days together, and this constituted an additional risk.

Before the loading was to begin, I could not help but notice all the elders who were in the prayer hall coming out and forming a sort of a chain. The truck was in position, and the loading of relief material was about to start. The elders would continue to pray as we loaded the truck. I had never experienced the power of prayer in this form. I realise now that prayer is of no use if it is not followed up with action. If the action consisted of human labour then prayer became that much more meaningful. It was late afternoon, Passang and his team were confident of making it back on the same day. All the volunteers got on to the truck and made themselves comfortable for the drive. The truck began to pull out of the Tibetan centre as the sound of prayers gradually drowned in the humdrum of traffic. Some prayers had been answered, and help was on its way.

CHAPTER 6

The Global and the Local

The nature of relief work is such that one must be selfless. May be they should let the APF (armed police force) take the relief to the people who need it. An idea such as this needs a little help to be digested. If the administration had paid attention to this, why were large swathes of the population left hungry? After all it had been almost ten days since the first earthquake had caused destruction. If the volunteers did not trust the APF, could they trust the administration? There were also stories of corruption that were doing the rounds. There was anger with the government, because everybody believed that they could be the ones obstructing relief efforts and doing very little on their own.

As resentment against the authorities increases, the relief work continues. It is a long road ahead, it seems straight and easy to navigate for now, it feels smooth but it is only a matter of time before the tarmac disappears. Driving a truck in this part of the world requires a driver to have a high level of skill, but for Bikash it is just another day. It is during times such as these, that his job becomes all important. There are several truck drivers like Bikash, all of whom are entrusted with the task of reaching different corners of Nepal with food and other aid supplies. Many lives are dependent on their service; they are the quiet unsung heroes of a nation in crisis.

As I continue to travel to the remotest parts of Nepal, the beginning of the journey is filled with a lot of hope. There were trucks bearing the symbols of the World Food Program (WFP), OXFAM, and other wings of the United Nations. It almost made me believe that soon we would not be required to carry out relief operations. This was a good sign simply because I had spent four days in Nepal now and this was the first time I could see progress after the issue over the Government of Nepal asking foreign nationals from thirty-three countries to leave the country. The intentions of the government, I felt were noble as they wanted the local community to take over all relief operations. However, my fellow companions did not share the same optimism; I would soon find out why.

The journey to what was assumed to be Malta in Lalithpur district was scenic. As soon as we got to the foothills, we were asked to stop by an APF check post. The officials at the post were asking the volunteers to fulfil 'unnecessary' obligations. 'It is getting hard to carry out relief work also', remarked one of the volunteers. The reason the administration had put such restrictions were simple. There were cases wherein relief volunteers had faced incidents of violence, and rules and permissions were put in place to protect the volunteers.

There are several reasons as to why people had turned wild while receiving relief. 'When people are coming to help, it is not right for the Nepali people to turn violent', said a volunteer. We all agreed, but perhaps there is another question that needed to follow the first question. Why did the people of Nepal in these untoward incidents turn violent? The answer was to be found in the place I was visiting. We did take long at the check point, at a certain point we wondered if this was to be the end of this operation. The police were suggesting that we leave all the relief with them and they would distribute as needed. The volunteers at no point trusted the Nepali government. They had a fair demand, after all it was their hard work that helped fund the relief material, it was their hard work with sourcing the material, they had packed and loaded each bag or rice, dhal, and cooking oil. Why should they lose the opportunity to bring their tasks to fruition?

Arguments and phone calls did the rounds until a determined band of volunteers gained the necessary permissions and the trucks carried on. All the bigger trucks of the UN, OXFAM, etc., had disappeared by now. The other relief trucks we saw belonged to groups of local volunteers. The presence of local volunteers on the ground was clear, but whatever happened to the guys at the UN and other global organisations, I wondered. The road by now had got from bad to worse. Some points were so narrow that it made me wonder if the truck could get stuck. At some point, I knew it was a miracle that we stayed on the road. The big trucks of the global organisations would not have made the journey, simply because the roads were way to narrow for them. The choice of truck made by the local volunteers of the RTYC seemed to be perfect. Or was it?

After hours of travel, we had still not reached Malta. We were not even close to our destination. We had missed the deadline to be at the first distribution point and the sun was packing up rather quickly. The problem, we realised rather late, was the rather vague administrative district segregations. Lalithpur was so big that the volunteers did not know where it started and how far it went. And these were people who had lived in Nepal all their lives!

We approached the slopes that would take us to our next distribution point. The small truck reflected in the feeble dying light of dusk, sputtered and stalled. The truck was too heavy for the volunteers to push it up. As soon as we managed to push it up a small distance, it would stall again and roll back the incline. We tried to improvise and would put a big stone under the truck so that it would not roll back and slowly, painstakingly made it over the steep slope. Providing relief in these parts was indeed a big task for small groups such as the RTYC, and I realised why these were the only people who could deliver relief in these areas.

I do not know why the larger organisations could not get to areas like Malta in Lalithpur. It brings me to the question, why did the people turn violent when organisations had gone to distribute aid? Firstly, relief material had been delivered very, very late. To add to this, the mix of material was not right kind. Let us take, for example, the distribution of biscuits to folk that need rice and pulses. More importantly, the relief they were carrying was insufficient to feed all the families in the area covered. When these factors are combined, can we blame people for tuning violent? Haven't we seen scavengers fight with animals for food that is rotting in the dustbins of all major cities in the sub-continent? So if we know the importance of food in ordinary times, are we not guilty of being alien to the feelings of hunger that was growing in the stomachs of our sisters and brothers, in a crisis situation.

As I got back on to the truck, in the midst of all the darkness that surrounded me, I remembered all the times I had put my faith in a large multinational branded organisation to be more responsible and respecting of my needs, simply because they had access to vast avenues of resources. Our little group had nothing. Not even the assurance that the truck would get us to our destination. But we did not care, for us there was light at the end of the tunnel. It is true that relief work should be selfless, it does not matter who distributes that relief. But a volunteer is human at the end of the day; she/he requires some fuel to continue their work. Perhaps that fuel is provided by the smile on an old woman's face, an old man, or child's gleeful laughter. Three kilograms of rice, dhal, and cooking oil can create magic; it brings out a smile that one can share with the inky darkness, perched atop a rickety truck, hurtling down a slope. It also gives you a good night's rest even when the ground beneath you begins to shake.

In retrospect, the remote areas should have food air dropped to them. Most did receive aid that was air dropped, but some remotes locations did get missed. If the local organisations had missed them, we could understand why. After all, there was this big information gap among organisations. The larger organisation cannot be excused. They had all the relevant data that was needed to make sure aid was given not only to every area but to every individual living in the remotest parts of Nepal.

CHAPTER 7

Behind Everything There Are Women and Men

W hen people tell you the best time of your life is the time you were a child, accept it and cherish it if it has not yet passed. If it has passed then you reminiscence over the past and think of how beautiful life was. At times I think of the past and I find regret, simply because I feel there were so many opportunities that I lost out on. I went to an all-boys school, and I never had the opportunity to work with a girl as an equal. With the passage of time, I have been lucky to find myself in the company of several women. Thanks to the company, I have had the pleasure of discussing several topics with girls from all age groups. There have been issues of safety, rape, dressing sense, and all the other issues that concern women.

Yeshi Choden barely sleeps these days. It is another tiring day, and the fact that she experienced tremors twice the previous night has not helped. There is something about Yeshi everybody around her will acknowledge; her energy levels drive everything and everybody around her. Not even an earthquake can quell her energy! She is a woman of conviction. Perhaps that is why she finds mention many times in this book. Yeshi holds the position of a general secretary in the RTYC Kathmandu Chapter. She has been instrumental in selecting the areas where relief would go. At times the volunteers wonder why she likes remote areas. Yeshi smiles and says 'What is the use of going to a place that has already received some kind of aid?'. With that, all discussions are put to rest.

It is a hot afternoon, and the truck has been stopped to give itself, the volunteers, and the driver a break. There are snacks served, and the mood in the camp is bright. Yeshi sits on a wall as she munches on her snacks. The ground begins to move rather violently. It is nothing compared to the previous tremors. Yet, she seems to be shaken more than all of us. There have been several instances where I have seen an incident shake Yeshi. What is inspiring is how her spirit copes. While there are some of us who recover fast, others like Yeshi are more sensitive and take some time to come around. One thing we can be certain off, once Yeshi is back on her feet and it is only a matter of time before everyone is up and ready to get going. It is a remarkable trait that she possesses to get everyone charged up and raring to go. It is so important for someone like her to be around. She gives the idea of women a whole new meaning, especially if you are coming from a background where we are always trying to figure out why women are treated as inferior to men instead of being perceived as equals.

All these issues and their aftermath always found a place in my quiet moments. Yeshi and her friends at the RTYC helped me see the difference between the girls in my friends circle and the girls in the Tibetan community. I will demonstrate with the help of an innocuous little incident. One of the most monotonous and taxing times in a relief operation is the packing of relief material. There were three different roles that were required. The first was to, pull out a portion of rice grain from a sack, hold a bag so that the grain could be put into it, and lastly tie the sack. If we had to do this in the south of India, where I come from, the subtle shifts in gender would have been at play. Apportioning the quantity of rice would have been largely viewed as a female role, whereas tying up the sack and transporting it would have been a masculine role. Of course exceptions would exist in pockets, but in general, tasks would be broken down in a group by culturally perceived gender-centric roles. This Nepali community was different. At no time during my stay, did I feel the guys in the group express an attitude that made me feel, they thought the job was demeaning of their masculinity.

When a sack of rice was emptied, someone had to go to fetch a new one. But the decision of who should get the bag was not determined by gender. It was determined by who was free at the time and taking a break or simply by who was closest to the bag. At times it would be the girls who brought in the reinforcements and just as often it would be the boys. At this point, I felt I was reading way too much into this situation. I am sure you are thinking the same. So I decided to introspect and identify my own cultural impulses. I noticed that while I did not feel any hesitation in holding the bag or tying the bags, when it came to pouring the rice into the bag I instinctively shied away. Could this have been because I felt it was more of a feminine role? Unfortunate as it may seem, I think I felt that way and so I decided I would deliberately only perform this task from then on. I wonder how the group perceived this change of heart. But perhaps, they were too busy and hassled to notice.

Once the packing of relief material was done, everybody got to work. This time the job was to load sacks of rice into the relief truck. While all the guys stepped up, the girls swung into action as well with the same enthusiasm and dedication. Sure at times the bags were a little too heavy and they needed a hand. Remarkably they did not complain, they just got together and shared the burden. As for my friend Yeshi she would not shy away from carrying the heaviest of bags. Yeshi's heroics do not stop here, she has put aside gender to push many a truck over steep hills. She has stood shoulder to shoulder with the other boys and girls of her group in every task, trial, and trouble.

At certain points in our life, all of us believe that certain roles are only for the men and some roles are limited to the women around us. These attitudes mostly reflect our culture and upbringing. If we do consciously correct our attitudes and determine a new course for our community and culture at large wouldn't we be hypocrites preaching equality? Could a girl ask for equality when she expects a boy to do the hard work without attempting to do it? The reason why I stress on attempting a task is important. An attempt may result in success or failure, but these are not determined by gender, rather more my attitude, determination, and persistence. Boys will fail and so will women and that is why we must all help each other, irrespective of gender or religion or culture.

CHAPTER 8

The City and the Village

Kathmandu is a simple yet beautiful city. Unfortunately, in the aftermath of the earthquake, it was no longer a tourist paradise. I had taken in very little of the local sights, though I had spent almost five days in Nepal now. The mission of our little group of volunteers was to mobilise relief for people affected by the earthquake in some of Nepal's remote villages. The only time we spent in the capital city Kathmandu was to plan and source the necessary material.

On one particular evening, we finished packing relief material quite late. I usually went to my sleeping quarters with Passang on his bike, but this time, he had a few chores to run and so I decided to get home on my own. I got out of the Tibetan centre and began to make my way to the local bus stop. I realised, I was in the touristy (Boudha) part of town, with some time to kill and so I began to take a walk in one of Kathmandu's most commercial areas.

I visited the Boudha Stupa (Place of worship for the Buddhists) and decided to take a look. Everything about the Stupa was fascinating to say the least. There were bands playing. They called it music for change. All around there were prayers and activities by groups trying to raise funds for the survivors of the earthquake. I did not realise how time had passed and it was almost late evening. I knew Kathmandu closed early but I did not know what that meant in terms of hours and minutes. It was close to 19.30 hours local time. I had spent an hour and half at Boudha gate. It was time for me to find a mini bus, but being late meant I had missed all the buses that would take me somewhere close to home. I knew the way home vaguely but was never a hundred per cent sure. The global positioning system on my phone would not work for some reason and I must admit I was fearful at that point.

After a long wait, I boarded a bus that would take me halfway to my destination. I spent a few nervous moments until I was dropped off at the last stop. I ran up to board another bus and a voice screamed out 'woh nahi jayega' which meant 'the particular bus will not go to my destination'. It was a man behind me who had begun walking briskly towards the main road. He stopped to tell me he was heading that same way and it would be half an hour's walk to get to Balaju Cholk. I looked around and could see that I lacked options. I should have left early. Nonetheless, it was pleasant outside. There was a slight drizzle in this envelop of darkness I found myself with. We began walking briskly, I reconfirmed the area we were heading to and realised I had was talking to a stranger. My stupidity had got me an interview with Sajit, a young man in his late twenties. We got talking and he asked me where I was from. I told him I was in Nepal as a relief volunteer. He seemed satisfied that I was just that and not another journalist looking for a human-interest story.

I had told Sajit about the areas I had visited and others I planned to be in. He was from the district of Gorkha that was badly hit during the earthquake. Sajit told me this was a bad time to be visiting Boudha as all the tourist places of interest were closed down. This he informed me, was because of a lack of manpower; people from the city had packed up and left to go to the villages. I immediately assumed this would be because of the damage the earthquake had caused. How wrong I was. Sajit asked me about a rumour that was doing the rounds; an earthquake was predicted that night. 'Why have you not left?' I asked him. He did not answer.

The rain was heavier now. We wondered if we should find some shelter or keep going. With very little to choose in terms of a sanctuary, we kept going. These are difficult days he said, one should not be out of his home and at the same time must not be indoors. An earthquake cannot be predicted accurately, I mused and people should not feed off each other's fear. Still, it may be best to leave the city and returned to the village temporarily. I did not know if was the rain on his face that caused his eyes to tear up. What he said was going to keep me awake all night.

Gorkha had been battered by the earthquake. Sajit's house went down taking the lives of his father and brother. He was the last male member of the family. Half of Kathmandu has gone back to the villages. They had not gone back because they feared living in Kathmandu but more because they were burdened by duty. They were going back to bury the dead and pay their last respects to people who they had loved or grown up with. The earthquake had traumatised the entire nation. One cannot experience it by merely walking through the ruins of Kathmandu. It could only be sensed in these quiet heartfelt conversations. The rain had much worse and made walking difficult. Every passing vehicle threw up a large splash of muddy water that drenched us. We had just crossed a refugee centre, and to our surprise, there was a woman selling tea at the corner.

I offered to buy Sajit tea. He was reluctant and offered to pay. In the traditions of the sub-continent, I did not relent and had my way. The shelter was overrun by people displaced by the earthquake and we had a lot of company in our warm corner of a shelter. As we sipped our hot tea, they enquired about me. Sajit joked that I had come to help although at the moment he was helping me to get home. As the conversation continued, Sajit told us he came back because there was a shortage of people at work. He worked in a restaurant where people had to be there. He had no choice now that he needed the money more than ever. We discussed the rumoured earthquake. At this point, one of the men got very vocal. He proclaimed he would leave the city tomorrow. 'If we are going to die, then I will die among the company of my family, friends, and loved ones'.

We wished the men well and continued down the dark lonely road. 'Who knows where is the safest place is for us?' Sajit said philosophically. 'It is true that fewer houses had fallen in the city when compared to the villages. But if I had to die, I would prefer to die with my family in the village. The houses are stronger here, but if it is cracked, there is nowhere to run. The buildings will fall on you. In the village, the houses will fall but there are open spaces. The truth is when it was time to die we have to die'.

We were almost at the end of our journey now. Balaju Cholk could be seen in the distance. There was palpable relief in my face. I thanked Sajit for the company and the assistance he had so willingly extended. He replied he was thankful for my efforts and others like me. 'We help each other', I remarked. We smiled at each other. He continued to walk straight up the road while I turned left; both of us were walking into the darkness not knowing what the night had in store for us.

CHAPTER 9

The Staircase

Days passed and nobody had visited him, but how would Ritesh know if people were looking for him. How would anyone know to look for a little lost boy of ten years in an emergency shelter? As the dust from the earthquake began to settle down, Ritesh and many others we gazing with stark fear at the vast unfamiliar sea of faces that peered at them and tried to find out who they were and where they belonged. When will he go back to the comforting warmth of his home and family, he must wonder. Ritesh is reluctant to talk to anyone around here. He sits all day in a corner avoiding contact with any aid workers or his peers. Tenzing Dolma works at this centre that has been taking care of these little children since the earthquake hit Nepal. She has been here since the day young Ritesh walked into the shelter home. She informs me that Ritesh does have relatives still living in Nepal; unfortunately, his immediate family was not able to survive the earthquake.

The relatives had told Tenzing that the boy was a cheerful boy of ten before the crisis struck. She is aware that the shock and trauma of being pulled out from the rubble of his home has turned Ritesh into a pale shadow of his former self. As a lecturer, I always fancied my ability to break the ice with young people fairly quickly. I thought I could get Ritesh talking, and so with Tenzing's permission, I walked up and sat on the ground, close by. The boy did not so much as acknowledge my presence. I had seen enough death and destruction by now and could begin to sense the extent of his loss. I could empathise with the people I had talked to in the course of my work.

Usually I would try the traditional way of starting a conversation. I asked him his name, he ignored me. I told him my name and that I was a teacher, there was no flicker or response. The child's lack of attention disturbed me. It felt like trying to talk to a stone. It had been a hard night and I had very little sleep. I could not find the energy to try something different with Ritesh. I lowered my bag on to the ground, seated myself comfortably and rested my head against the wall and tried to sleep. To my surprise, this managed to draw some reaction from Ritesh. He turned his head to look at me. In normal circumstances, this would have been a good sign, for it would symbolise a beginning; with Ritesh, the expression said 'you are invading my space'.

I realised the boy needed some quiet, and there was very little I could do to help him. Perhaps allowing him the peace of his tiny corner was the only thing he needed for now. In the meantime, some of the other children had come back after a game of football. They left the ball close to us and headed towards the showers. Football has been a childhood passion, and I could never resist the urge to tackle an idle ball lying around. I began to dribble and in a short while the ball had bounced away in the direction of Ritesh. He did not let the ball pass; he juggled a bit and kicked it back to me. I invited to him to an impromptu game; he scowled and lapsed back to his corner. I then began kicking the ball against the wall beside which he was seated. Occasionally the ball would roll over to him. At may be the fifth attempt, he came forward to pass the ball to me. In the next fifteen minutes, Ritesh would display his footballing prowess, which was pretty impressive for a child his age.

I told him I was from Bangalore and asked him if he would like to come visit me. He looked at me and said, he wanted to go back to his own house. I offered to do this. He replied 'nahi hai' which meant 'not there'. I did not ask him to elaborate for fear of upsetting him. An awkward silence followed. I asked him if he would be kind enough to show me around the building, and to my surprise, he readily agreed. While we were walking, I gently brought the conversation around to the topic of home. A teary eyed, frightened-looking Ritesh acknowledged, for perhaps the first time, that there would probably be no home for a long time.

I put my arm around the boy as the tears begun to flow. What was I to do to comfort him; crack a joke and lighten the moment or wait while the bottled emotions found its sorrowing expression? 'What do you remember about home?' I asked the boy. He wiped his tears and began to describe his home with vivid gestures, as only children can do. 'Mine was a big house', he said grandly. 'Everybody visited us'. The house was famous for its staircase, designed and built by his grandfather, who took great pride in his handiwork. The stairwell was adorned with pictures of generations of the family. It stood in mute testament of their progress and growth.

Ritesh was at home when the earthquake had struck his house. He had been tucked away under a table at the back end of the wall. It was the eastern side of the house that had taken the hit where the family was cowering. As he was rescued, he recalls watching his neighbours take out a body; he did not know who it was. The broken body of his grandfather lay at end of the broken staircase. Ritesh worries he will never see his beloved home again. He remembers his own pictures that hung in the house and the many games, a multitude of friends, cousins, and relatives had joyously concocted for their youngest treasure.

One of the games he fondly recalled was playing 'chor–police' or 'Cops and Robbers' with his mother or grandfather. The grills of the staircase were turned into a jailhouse where he would gleefully imprison the 'robbers'. Ritesh always played the police man. It was ironic that these little moments would forever imprison his innocent childhood. The faces of his family were forever imprisoned behind the grills of the staircase, calling out to Ritesh, asking their little tormentor to let them out.

Will Ritesh overcome this tragedy? Will he heal enough to piece together a stair, step by step that will take him beyond the prison of memory? Perhaps in time, he will! The age-old question of why some are chosen for more difficult life paths than others rears its ugly head. What could possibly justify the loss of innocence in young victims of a natural disaster of this scale? Who would they learn to blame? The answers to these questions are not with Ritesh or us. The nature of death is such that it alters the lives of the living. Shouldn't we spare a moment each day to think about the millions who suffer Ritesh's fate? Be happy for what we have but not forget those out there who need our empathy and support.

As I walked out of the shelter, the unfairness of it all left a bitter aftertaste. I began to wonder why, I was here.

To help perhaps, but what assistance could we offer young Ritesh? All our hopeful utterances, sounded hollow even to our adult, trained ears. It is in moments like this that we question our purpose as volunteers, trained or untrained. To hold the hands of a victim, young or old, look in their eyes and share that moment of silent, hopeless frustration is perhaps a relief when the world is going crazy around you.

CHAPTER 10

The Man Who Didn't Die

The importance of time is paramount in the ranges surrounding the Himalaya. Once the sun goes down, the extent of darkness is staggering. Every now and then the silence is broken by the music of nature or the roar of passing airplane. At times one wonders why the planes fly so low, not realising the many thousands of feet above sea level over which Nepal stands. While the darkness may be a treat for spiritually inclined, it spells bad news for any other practical purpose. One of the biggest problems

45

we encountered in conducting relief work in remote areas, located in the Himalayas, is of distance. Homes are set far apart from each other and a neighbourhood can be spread over many miles Getting to these remote areas is also a herculean task and very rarely accomplished in a scheduled time span.

Once the sun sets, it becomes difficult for the village folk to gather at a particular point. Most often some of them will turn up while others never show. The group has to tread with care in these circumstances because a misplaced word or action can lead to violence. After travelling days and surmounting physical and mental odds, a volunteer wants nothing more than to deliver supplies to the people who need it. The logistical challenge of ensuring everyone in the designated area has received supplies limit the volunteer group options. Either get the word out for everybody to be at a common point and leave unclaimed relief material with the army or go down to each of the houses and deliver supplies. The choice is mostly one dictated by the geography of the neighbourhood.

It had been a fairly regular day. Our little group of volunteers had delivered food supplies to a village and were making their way towards another village. We had just negotiated a steep incline and were on the lookout for a place to catch a quick breath. We traded stories and talked about how unprepared we were for this journey and our learnings along the way. As they walked through the quiet fields, we met a man who immediately began screaming and creating a nuisance. I was surprised and a little scared as I had no idea what had set him off. The Nepali he spoke made it difficult for me to understand his tirade. The women prepared to defend themselves in case the man got more aggressive.

Somewhere in the middle of the garbled monologue, I realised the man was crying. We had by now edged past him and the stench of alcohol reached us. 'There is no food here, but there will always be alcohol', my friend joked. But, then again wouldn't that be the same everywhere in the world. There was no time to dwell on how and where the man procured his stash. We put our bags down and listened. My friends translated for me.

The man was angry with God and was cursing both God and himself. What was he so angry about? He survived the earthquake, while his family perished. At first, this may seem ungrateful. If you looked at the firefighters and rescue force trying to dig babies and children out from under the rubble, they would at times find that the cause was a lost one from the start. Yet refusing to give up, to these people who have made protecting life their personal motto, this seemed like a rather sad reward. Scratch the surface and look at the man's story like so many others across the country, it came with a sting. How does one protect the will to survive? How does one contemplate life without the presence of family and friends? Is living in a perpetual state of grief worth the trouble?

By now we were used to the fact that we try as we may to provide sustenance for the body, there was very little comfort we could provide for scarred memories and grieving souls. Yet, these experiences stayed with us, invaded our subconscious mind and returned to haunt us in the tired moments when we sought the healing elixir of sleep. They came back in our nightmares and any quiet moment of contemplation. Heavier than the rucksacks of food we carried, these burdens of thought weighed on our minds.

As our sober group began our journey again, I thought of Sajit and Ritesh. They were faced with the formidable task of starting again. Perhaps Ritesh would find it a tad bit easy, a child's ability to adapt asserting itself, but what about this man and other men like him? What would happen to them? They had passed the prime of their lives. All their dreams and hopes had revolved around their families and children. May be they would seek the succour of the locally produced spurious liquor for a while. Someday even its numbing comfort will desert them. What then? Where would these broken minds and hearts seek comfort then?

This man who railed against God and the world had reminded me and my Nepali friends that the reconstruction of Nepal would not be all about buildings and infrastructure. Finding solace for broken minds and bodies would be paramount. Deadlines can be set and resources procured to rebuild a fallen landmark. But rebuilding a torn life would take more patience, love, and empathy from a weary nation. Personally, it reminded me how much we take the presence of family and friends for granted. How little of our own existence we can tolerate without the understanding and assistance of our loved ones. Life indeed is a burden, if not lightened up by the warm presence of those that bring a smile to our hearts even in the dreariest moment.

CHAPTER 11

Finding Faith

To be religious or not has never been the question. Understanding the followers of organized religion, on the other hand, is something that has become both a private and global pastime. It is a topic that can invite fanatic outbursts, quite philosophy, contempt, disdain or plain indifference; the latter being more common nowadays as proclaimed by many fashion accessories.

My own position is a bit of a grey area. Having been born and bought up in a devout Catholic family, I haven't had the courage to completely throw away the observations or traditions of my religion. I have at different times rebelled but have never managed to cut ties or become the convert – my mother would love to see.

History and newspapers are rife with evidence of religion being the crutch by which man inflicts his or her most nefarious intentions. Every day some innocent is tortured, maimed, or killed either because they belong or do not belong to a certain religion. No other topic has the power to polarize the most laid back person as religion. One insensitive sentence can turn a priest into a butcher of men.

In the aftermath of the earthquake in Nepal, social media was rife with all kinds of opinions, posts, and surveys about the relevance of God in the face of a natural disaster. One online post on Facebook read 'Do we pray to the same God who had the power to make sure the earthquake did not happen in the first place?' When over 10,000 people were feared, it seemed rather naïve to have a philosophical debate on whose job it was to prevent such natural disasters. The best everyone in the world outside Nepal could do was pray and donate money. It seemed quite frustrating and hopeless.

It was one of the factors that influenced my journey to Nepal as a volunteer with the relief effort. Along the way, I had to conquer my fears of leaving the boundaries that surrounded me since birth – my country, family and friends, even my prejudice and opinions. I was just a tiny, little speck in the universe. Now on my own, with a growing awareness that the world was more immense and more complex than my imagination. Though air travel has shrunk distances and distant places are now accessible in days, the barriers of culture, language, and our basic human nature remain as strong and insurmountable as always. Family and friends were supportive, but one could see the worry lines crease my mother's smile as she wished me a safe return. I would remember that smile many times during the course of my stay in Nepal; a memory that would comfort, trouble, and even strengthen. A smile indeed has immense power.

At the Tibetan centre, which acted as command centre for the RYTCE earthquake relief efforts, I witnessed a different form of spirituality. The idea of prayer coupled by action appealed to me immensely. It was overwhelming to see older members of the community engage in prayer for victims and their families. While the young and the able went about raising awareness about the immediate needs of affected populations, mobilizing and delivery relief material to families in far-flung areas. Hard work must always bring some result. But it took more than hard work to reach some of the areas we mapped out for our efforts, and with our limited resources, we needed some luck and a great deal of grace. The emotional toll that people's grief took on our young group was also quite a challenge. It was depressing work for most part. There was no joy to be found even when we managed to reach a destination. So many victims wanted to join their families. But then along would come a child, we would kick some dust around, play a game. We would find some young families, grateful for supplies and hopeful of starting again, some of the old, who would smile and bless us in passing. And just like that our weary souls and spirits would be replenished, and we would find the energy to climb another hill, walk a few more miles, and even face our fears when the ground shook beneath our weary feet.

I was accustomed to the idea that charity meant lightening your wallet while feeling a pang for the snack or meal that one was planning for at a favourite restaurant. It meant braving boring home-cooked food or giving up time with friends over beer and television. The small 'sacrifice' meant someone, somewhere had fewer tears to contend with, a meal to eat or a bed for the night; maybe even writing materials and a uniform to attend classes in a concrete building with some well-intentioned teacher brightening the future of the world. It was a good thought to sleep on at night; changing the world by a snack at a time. Awake, the newspapers were rife about nuns being raped, churches burnt, statements and counter statements that fuelled more hatred and mistrust. Very rarely would one wonder if the people our well-intentioned charity was meant for even existed. That maybe the price of social freedom, mobility, and education meant a frightening death. That maybe there was no one to funnel charity to the most deserving, because the price of a meal meant brutal repercussions on the whole family or community. It seemed to make sense to worship at the altar of individualism and capitalism.

Nepal changed that for me. It helped break the cynicism that soured by mind and tongue when I heard about a charitable effort. To be able to communicate a sense of hope with my packets of food and water, I realized I needed to have some of my own. I could only channel my own hope to people who looked at me with despair. I forgot self in my pursuit to reach another village, another town. For the first time in my life, I spent a large part of my day without thinking about myself. Had I become spiritual? To loose oneself in the attainment of a higher awareness was the path to spirituality, or so I had heard. But these were not thoughts that occurred then.

It was never a good time in Nepal; a smile could turn into a tear faster than a bright sunny day turned gloomy. In fact, the number of disappointments was far greater than our achievements. I am reminded of an instance when all the relief volunteers of the RTYC were en route to a place known as Jiri (The Switzerland of Nepal, as it is better known as). It had been a hard day unlike any other. The morning sun had beatened us mercilessly, by late noon, we were soaked to the bone by driving rain, yet we were happy that we did not have to get of the truck and push it up the slopes. Yes, we were happy we had better equipment that day. All of a sudden, there was a bang, as the driver of the truck hit the right front tyre of the truck into the wall of the hill we were climbing. Had he gone to the left side of the road, there would have been no wall but the slopes of the valley, 300 feet below was the river. There was no chance of survival if we had to go down that path.

We were stranded in the remotest parts of Nepal, with nowhere to go. The truck could not be abandoned simply because it was carrying food for around 500 families that had not seen relief for close to eleven days after the first earthquake. It was dark and the road was abandoned. Most of our phones were out of coverage area. The driver of the truck could not put the truck back into working conditions. As some of us sat by the corner of the road and awaited a decision from the leaders on what could be done? It was then decided that some of us would stay with the truck, while the others would move out and try to get help in the form of another vehicle if possible.

While we moved to get help, the ground beneath us began to move. The mud under those of us on the side of the valley began to slide into the river. We could hear our friends beside the truck scream, but none of us did, maybe because we did not expect to survive. At that point, my mother's smile flashed vividly across the valley, I remember thinking it was a good thought to be buried alive in. Once everything stood still again, in my heart I found myself calling out to the power that was watching over me. A few minutes passed in silence. The earth seemed to have settled down. My fellow volunteers found unique ways of distressing themselves. While some of them lit a cigarette, the other read verses from holy books. In our own ways, we found the strength to carry on. Now with more conviction, we had found a reason to carry on our journey, fight the odds that were stacked against us. We were needed to serve the God who stood in lines to collect food grain, pulses, and oil. God was everywhere, in everything.

I was reminded of this moment, a few days later at a programme organized in church. It was supposed to be an occasion where people from all regional and linguistic backgrounds were asked to pray together. The result was not entirely surprising, as people who spoke English did not want to waste time in associating themselves with people who aligned themselves with other lingual backgrounds. I was disappointed but not surprised as I knew I was back home and people here followed a different system disguised as religion.

CHAPTER 12

Mama's Coming Home

Lalith packs his bagpack, he is carrying relief for a family of four. A third-year-degree-student Lalith is inspired by a belief that tells him he is an agent of change. 'We live for ourselves in the city, we feel responsible for our families only. What happens to the people who help society function, don't we have a responsibility towards them? I understand these are just things we would like to talk about. I feel I have spoken enough, and Nepal was an opportunity for me to do something. That was what I felt five days back, when I left', he has a cheeky smile on his face but as the weight of his bag makes its presence felt, he comes back to reality. It will be a seven-six kilometre trek, and Lalith may take close to an hour to reach his destination.

Gorakhpur, a settlement in the district of Gorkha; the land is famous all over the world because history has branded it as the land of the brave. The pride and honour of the gorkha's (as they are commonly known) can be felt in the little time spent with them. People of this region are hardworking people, they thrive on completing challenges that other people would commonly term as silly. The earthquake along with repeated tremors had made rescue and relief work in the area hard. Gorakhpur was a minefield of challenges, the tasks given to the volunteers seemed silly and unthinkable.

Houses in the area are not situated close to each other; rather they are located at length and that makes distribution of relief material a challenge. Under normal relief circumstances, the village representatives would be asked to assemble all individuals at a particular spot, at a particular time, so threat relief could be distributed. The same strategy was adopted but the local representatives informed the volunteers that it would be difficult to implement the same strategy. Hence, the volunteers packed their bags with relief materials and set off in different direction. Most of the relief destinations were at best a two-and-a-half-hour walk from the relief truck. The idea behind such a strategy was to help injured people clear debris and set up make shift shelters for the affected family.

With every volunteer armed with relief material and a destination. The group split up and headed in their respective destinations. It was late afternoon with very little time left before the rays of the sun disappear. Since the day begins early, the day felt longer than normal. At times the high temperatures resulted in volunteers suffering from sun burns. The occasional thunder showers in the afternoon did not provide respite; it only made life difficult for us. Luckily we were joined by the members of the National Cadet Corpse for this operation. I would not want to place too much of importance on the ideas that may arise from a brand such as the NCC. As this would be a grave injustice to the many ordinary people working as volunteers in Nepal. Yes, these are citizens who are trained and were able to help a great deal with the relief work. However, every individual made a substantial contribution in providing relief. On a lighter note, perhaps it is the conditions of Gorkha that brings courage to the women and men of Gorakhpur.

It is a picture perfect landscape but there is little time to admire nature's paintings. Lalith will choose to go off-road at times so as to cut short his journey. There is immense pressure to reach the allotted destination. Lalith has been in Nepal for a total of five days now; he has gained a lot of experience in clearing debris. On the way, he must make his way through settlements that have been brought down to the ground by the earthquake. The view is breath taking even for Lalith, who has seen his share of destruction for a long time now. Once he reaches his destination, Lalith empties his rations rather quickly, as most of the people had gathered in an orderly manner. The people were thankful for the food he had brought along with him. Lalith noticed the number of hands needed to clear the debris is not enough. Since he had time on his hands, he offered to help.

'I have seen so many houses broken because of the earthquake; I have even entered a few. Yet, when I am called up to help clear houses for the ones who are not able to do so, I am filled with so much emotion, that life becomes hard'. The houses on the top of the foot hills of the Himalayas are not very strong buildings; they are commonly known as 'Kacha makans'. These are houses that are made with mud, stone, and some wood fused together. There is no chance of such buildings surviving an earthquake of this magnitude.

Once he had readied a checklist of people who are missing, presumed dead, alive and have received relief or alive but have not received any kind of aid. Lalith also enquired about people who are in need of medical assistance. 'There are two children here', Lalith informs me. 'We have to help them set up temporary shelters, if we do not do that; these fevers will become hard to deal with'. Lalith is right with his analysis of the situation. The weather conditions and the fear of epidemic run high in such situations. A mild fever can escalate into something else. It takes only a few minutes for a bright sunny day to turn into a misty drizzle or a thunder storm. The region has witnessed hard rains in the last few days after the earthquake, making relief work difficult.

Lalith usually prefers work that requires a certain level of labour. 'Yes! I can never see myself sitting at a desk from nine in the morning to five in the evening'. 'Out of all the work given to me, this is my favourite', he says with a smile. The smile lasts for a short while as he begins to move stones and mud with his hands. There is nothing much to retrieve from these houses, the only important thing is for us to retrieve the wood. The wood is the only valuable part of the house that can be re-used when the reconstruction begins. That is why there is a lot of wood that has been piled up on the sides of the roads. 'It is the only useful thing', as Lalith sees it.

While clearing mud and stone is the most rewarding relief work for Lalith, it is also the most traumatising of relief work. The problem with this kind of work is you never know what you will find beneath the layers of mud and stone. As the debris get cleared, they are increasingly scrutinised by people who own the property or people who are related to people who own the property. At times Lalith picks up things that may seem utterly useless to him, only to catch the ire of the eyes that scrutinise his work. In this instance, Lalith moves a broken wooden stand that is beyond repair and is utterly useless even to my eyes. All of a sudden he begins to realise he is drawing fire from an old lady screaming at him in Nepali. It is here that Lalith realises he is clearing one of the houses of a couple whose names are on his presumed dead list. The shock on Lalith's face is prominent; there is a sense of disbelief that will accompany him in the next few words that will come out of his mouth. He tries his level best to apologise to the lady as she breaks down into tears.

He understands it is a lost cause as he makes his way away from the ruin. There is no amount of consoling that can help either the old lady or Lalith.

With a heavy heart, he realises it is time for us to begin his journey back to the relief truck. Only this time, I notice a sense of weariness in Lalith footsteps. I understand it is pain and trauma that he has exchanged his bags of rice with. Yet, the journey back to the relief truck has to be made. It is a lonely walk for Lalith as no words are exchanged by him. With his head pointed down, Lalith makes his way out of the settlement. There is a lot going on in his head at this moment, there is no desire to look at the great Himalayan landscape for now. He makes it back to the relief truck where he finds his friends have had a better day.

With some tea available, Lalith decides to have some tea before the truck is ready to move out. He makes his way to wash his face before that cup of tea arrives. As the tea cups arrive, the volunteers are surrounded by children who are amazing at lightening up such moments. Soon there will be a lot of noise as volunteers begin to run and play with the children. There are children who are having a fun time with the volunteers but there are also those children who want to keep to themselves. Once he finishes his cup of tea, Lalith makes his way to leave his tea cup under a tree. He finds a group of children sitting beside the tree. Something feels wrong; he enquires why one particular boy was in tears. Had his friends bullied him? If yes, Lalith was going to redeem himself by being that boy's saviour.

Unfortunately, the children around this 'victimised' boy were only trying to help this boy cheer up. Lalith would soon learn that this was a boy who belonged to the same village from where he had come from. Lalith tells the boy he had been to his house only to find the boy look at him as a hero. With all the hope in his heart, the boy will now ask Lalith a question that Lalith is not prepared to answer.

A shocked Lalith is now trying his best to recall the data he had put together; in his heart, he knows he does not have the answers to the boy's questions. The shock and the tension of the moment do not let Lalith recall the names of people in any of his lists. Yet, he will answer the boy's first question Where is my mother, did you meet her? Lalith now has put on the most genuine of smiles on his face as he begins to respond to the boy. 'They were supposed to come today! But, the big house they are building for you is not yet complete. As soon as it is complete, they will come to take you and if you cry like this every day then they will take a longer to come'. 'Do you want that?' asks Lalith. The tears have now dried up, and the boy looks at Lalith with a blush on his face.

Lalith boards the relief truck as he is all set to leave. Tomorrow will be a well-earned rest day for Lalith and his team. There is a question that he will carry with him from here. Is the wood the only useful thing he clears from those houses? Or is it the memories that are represented in mud and stone.

CHAPTER 13

China, India, and Tibet

In the midst of the dark cold night sits a bleeding cow, there are tears rolling down her face. She is a victim, not of her own making but the unfortunateness that is called life. As she continues to struggle, there is help that arrives not because there is a want to help, but because there is something that can be gained in return for the help that is provided. As help from the south arrives in the form of a Tiger, a Dragon arrives from the north. What must she do? What can she do? How can she get herself to accept the help these creature have to offer? Whilst being aware that acceptance of any kind will mean the death of her freedom. This analogy comes good when compared to the situation Nepal found itself in. Both Nepal's government and its people are thankful to the Indian government and its people for the quick relief provided in the wake of the immediate aftermath of the earthquake. However, the politics that was played out under the guise of relief work was so bad that Nepal had eventually refused to take any kind of help or support from the Tiger (India).

The massive publicity campaign that India had attempted had backfired. This could have possibly handed over the initiative to the Chinese government, who even to this date continues to take the lead in whatever is required to be done in Nepal. This could be either providing relief, providing machinery to clear or rebuild any kind of infrastructure, assist with medical teams, and so on and so forth. The presence of the Chinese initiative is so large that it cannot be missed. Every refugee centre you visit in Kathmandu or areas surrounding Kathmandu, you will notice very well-built tents and canopy's bearing the logo of the People's Republic of China. The Chinese Reportage was not all glamorous but focused on work being done by their governmental organisations. It was factual as it should be, was it unbiased or biased is for the people to judge. Of course people must not expect much when the media is owned by the state.

It was clear that both the Indian and Chinese government were busy playing politics, each trying their level best to influence a Nepali government that is perhaps still in its early days. Both the Indian and Chinese government very well knew that the local government had internal problem. The people of Nepal were angry with the government simply because they believed that it was not doing enough for the people at a time when they needed assistance the most. A few days after the frenzy had reduced, the Nepali government asked foreign nationals from thirty-three countries to leave Nepal. The idea behind such a move was logical; the government wanted all relief operations to be taken over by local groups and communities. The problem to such an idea, however, was the fact that there was no system in place which could be used by local relief operations. The result was chaos in relief work coupled with the fact that local organisations found it difficult to conduct rescue and relief operations.

In this political ball game, perhaps the biggest loser is the Nepali government itself. This is simply because as a new democracy, the government was presented with a fine opportunity to convince the people of Nepal about democracy as a system. The failure of the government to do so has resulted in questions being raised about the future of this government. The second biggest loser could be the Indian government. The failure of the Indian governments diplomacy was clearly evident on the streets of Nepal. In the ten days that I travelled across Nepal, I did meet a few Indian relief workers, but these were either from the NGO sector or missionaries. The only Indian flag I saw was on the occasional air planes around the airport of Kathmandu. In contrast to this, the biggest winner for me personally was the People's Republic of China. There was at least one canopy which bore the symbol of the Chinese army. There were medical centres on the road that bore the symbol of the Chinese. It was the best use of soft power I had ever seen and it did work! The people of Nepal were indebted to the Chinese, they looked at them as saviours and warmed up to them; there were no hard feelings when the Chinese army took charge of any operation, the people of Nepal did co-operate with them.

The Chinese influence was so great that by the time the wings of the United Nations and other world programmes had only managed to set up a network to distribute rations, the Chinese government had already begun with road works. One of the problems, when it came to building infrastructure and clearing roads in the remote areas was that the heavy machinery could not make it to these areas. The roads were too narrow to transport them. Even then the Chinese department of public work had managed to bring in heavy machinery to these isolated locations. The speed at which these organisations completed their work was commendable.

Now it had been close to seven or eight days in which I had spent a lot of time with my friends in the Tibetan community. There was much to learn from them, there was also this pain they were accustomed to living with. The pain of not having a land to call their own, yet they continued to put their heads down and work. I have been for a while now, sympathetic to the Tibetan cause for freedom. As an individual with a masters in communication science, I do understand the importance of branding and public relation. It is because of this, I noticed the objective and importance of having logos and brand names on canopies and sacks carrying relief material. I also noticed the Tibetan folk did not have any structure put in place so that they can counter such forms of propaganda. Could they afford to ignore it; after all, they did have a score to settle with the Chinese. In the time spent with them, I could tell that the wounds of losing their motherland to the Chinese people were fresh. They did not like the Chinese government for all the atrocities committed in Tibet. Yet, they were not against the people of China. This was evident because one of the volunteers who had joined us on the operation at Jiri was Chinese! All of us got along well and everything worked out fine! What were the Tibetans thinking?

To me this was an opportunity to gain support from the Nepali people and the world at large. It was an opportunity to tell the world about a land known as Tibet. However, I was here just as an observer; I was not here to tell people how to do and what to do. Somehow, my helplessness got the better of me, and I asked Passang why he was not using this opportunity to fight against the Chinese. Passang took some time and then replied. What he said made me realise how shallow my thoughts were. He said 'This is not the time to play politics, People have died here, and the people of Nepal continue to suffer. They know it is the Tibetan community that has been giving them food. We are grateful to the people of Nepal for giving us a home and at this time of need, we want to show them that we will do whatever we can to help them'. Passang had made me realise that there was no difference in between me and the Indian media that I have been critical about. I was furious with myself for coming up with such ideas.

How many of us would think and act in accordance with the ideas of Passang? Not many, I am sure. Why is it that we have become so self-centred I thought to myself? Could it be the influence of my city life that had made me so individualistic? These are questions we must ask ourselves, above all we must have the ability to reflect and seek answers to questions such as these. We must then above all have the courage to correct our thought process. I believe the ideas and thought process possessed by Passang were worth more than gold. If my thinking had been altered by the urban environment I was surrounded by, then surely Passang's thinking was the product of his simple society. Will we be able to change; I do not know! But I know for certain we should, for to be human is to live with the ideas of the Tibetan community. To live in the way we continue to live is no different than living like a scavenger, feeding of the helpless. What use is the evolution of a human being if he continues to feed of another's misery?

I must clarify, my intention of writing this particular piece is not to critically examine the various governments in the picture. The purpose of writing this piece is to get individuals to introspect on our own doings. I wouldn't make the mistake of generalising, but I am sure most of us have been guilty while we donate to different causes. We do expect recognition for our contributions or to be treated differently. In our world of glamour, we must be critical of our own actions; after all we are the government.

CHAPTER 14

Democracy and Monarchy

One must never underestimate the use of bar tables in the local banal that give people space to consume alcoholic beverages. It is in these places and yes it is under the influence of alcohol, where one will find some of the most interesting conversations, debates, and discussions pertaining to all topics under the sun. Now as most of you would know, Nepal has been recovering from a very turbulent political past. Not long before were they being governed by a monarchy, today they have a very young democratic government governing them. The people of Nepal have been brought up with stories about kings, their heroic deeds, and their service to the kingdom. Interestingly, this is the season where most of the old folk of Nepal are telling both the middle-aged and young folk of how things unfolded under the king.

The closest people of my generation have got to living under a monarchy is in our text books. As historians would say, the history we study is not the most accurate recording of facts. The people of my generation in India have never been under any other form of government other than the corrupt, red-tapped democratic system. We were born under this system of governance and subsequently ended up following it. More problematically, we ended up following this system without being able to question if it was really the best system. Much of this problem perhaps remains in the cradle of our great and rigorous educational system. All along my journey to the remote areas of Nepal, right from the second day, I found myself in discussions about which form of governance was the best. There was some great participation as well! We had the American views being mixed with Indian, Tibetan, and Nepali views; all in all, this was a healthy mix under the intoxicating influence of country-brewed Nepali liquor.

There was a genuine lack of trust in democracy on the Nepali side, clearly as they would go on to demonstrate, they had better days. Monica a young student studying in a prestigious institution in Kathmandu goes on to narrate an incident that took place eighty years back. 'So you know every eighty years there is a big earthquake in Nepal right?' she pauses to see if her audience is with her, once she receives her confirmation she continues. So when the earthquake hit Nepal eighty years back, we had the king. The destruction was even greater but the king was there to instil hope among the people. He immediately sent water to all the parts of Nepal, even the remotest of remote parts. He addressed his subjects and told them to wipe their tears. The time had come for Nepal to rebuild herself. The people found hope in the leadership of the king and this resulted in the people of Nepal rebuilding their country.

The problems faced eighty years ago were not very different to the problems faced by the people of Nepal today. Tashi at this point adds to what Monica is saying. If you go to the small tuck shops outside the open spaces, where large refugee camps are situated, you will notice the price of a

Mari Biscuit packet which is close to thirty Indian Rupees is being sold for almost eighty Indian Rupees. How can people who have lost their livelihood and are living on the roads be expected to survive in such conditions? Without the aid, they are receiving it would be impossible. People in the remote areas have been able to survive for so many days without relief due to the fact that these areas give opportunities for food gathering. Tashi was right; people in the cities did not have the option of food gathering because they lived in a concrete jungle.

So how did the king solve this problem? Gregory, the American, enquires inquisitively? Tashi responds with a smile on his face. Hording was a problem eighty years back as well, but when the king got to know about merchants hoarding, he passed an order. If a person complained to the local authorities about a person hording and backed his claim with the help of five witnesses, the representatives of the king would cut off the head of the merchant.

Fear has always been a great way of controlling the masses; it was useful in times like these. Yet there is a problem with monarch as I pointed out. What would happen if the king was not a good leader? What if he was self-centred and did not care for the people. Monica was quick to jump on to that queue.

She began to narrate the incident not so long ago when the brother of the king was rumoured to have murdered the family of the king. The people resented him she reports, when there was a natural calamity a not so long back, the brother of the king who had taken the place of the king sent drinking water to the area of destruction. However, the people only used the drinking water to wash their hands. That was the problem with monarchy, as all of us seemed to agree; in a monarch, you were stuck with a king until he died! Until then, the people of the kingdom remained at the mercy of the king.

It was now our turn to sell democracy as an idea to the interested ones around us; interestingly, neither the Americans nor could I sell democracy as a form of good governance. We acknowledged that democracy as a system on paper was very different when compared to democracy as a system when practised. The problem for us was that we agreed over democracy being a system that legalised the control of capitalism on each and every one who came under its purview.

The discussions ended with the beginning of volunteer's falling asleep. It had been a pleasant night to star gaze. Well, there was a problem with that too; the height of the mountains that watched over us was so great that we could not tell which one was a star in the sky and which one was a house on the mountain. Why had we not discusses the other forms of governance I wondered. In our class rooms, we simply brushed these ideas a side. Oh yes, I remembered why we did not spend time discussing it. It wasn't in our syllabuses.

CHAPTER 15

The Problem of Rebuilding

As the rays of the sun begin to put aside the darkness, hope is scarce; will any relief come this way? It is time for the men in uniform to come on their routine rounds. 'They come every day but do nothing for us'. The APF of Nepal commands a great amount of respect amongst the people of Nepal. This statement is the beginning of a trust deficit that may result in the army losing some of its sheen. The root cause of such a statement can be traced to the fact that there have been accusations of corruption within the new Government of Nepal. There is also the fact that the flow of aid to these regions has been slow adding to the frustration of the people.

Rahul is in the third year of service with the APF, he has travelled to different areas affected by the earthquake collecting data for the Government of Nepal. His first task is to survey the building and depending on the strength of the building to withstand tremors, he allocates different colour-coded stickers. These stickers were coloured red, orange, or green. 'This initiative of the government to allot sticker codes saved a lot of lives in the past few days. If not in the villages, they certainly worked in the city'. Most of the houses that have been labelled red cannot be occupied, as any small tremor may bring it down causing death and destruction. After the identification of these houses, the next task is to provide people with temporary shelters. This is a very complex part in the process of rebuilding of Nepal.

Rahul's facial expressions are enough to tell you about the magnitude of the task at hand; just the other day, he had visited the house of a lady called Rashi. While he began the inspection of the house, Rashi had informed him that the house was constructed just two years ago. It was her dream house and the family had put in a lot of its life savings into the construction of the house. Rahul has been in this situation before, yet he was helpless. Rashi has been sleeping in the government school two streets away from her place; she recognises the fact that her house is not the safest place to get any sleep at night. However, she is hopeful that soon the ground beneath her feet will stop moving and she can return to her home. Once everything is settled, she plans on slowly fixing the cracks; she will not be able to do it immediately, because she does not have the money to do it now.

While Rahul patiently listens to what is being told to him, he knows her plans of rebuilding are not going to work; yet he must try and explain the problem to her. The house she lives in has been constructed around the pillar which developed a crack. To make matters worse, not one but three pillars including the central beam of the house has developed dangerous cracks. No amount of repair work can make the building safe he recognises.

While Rahul patiently explains the problem, Rashi remains in disbelief; most of the houses that have fallen have been old houses. The house she lives in is close to two years old surely it can be made proper with a few repairs, just like the other houses of the same age. Rahul tells her there have been at least a few thousand houses in Nepal, that are of the same age and have suffered the same fate. However, then he realises there is nothing much he can do to convince her about the house. He decides to label the house with an orange sticker and must continue to look at the other houses in the area. 'People like Rashi, it is not their fault. Building an own house in Kathmandu is not a joke. An own house here is a sign that your future is secure. Building a house in the city is not cheap and usually people empty everything they have to construct their houses'.

If the rumours are true and the Government of Nepal does decide on giving people who have lost houses some kind of aid. How much will the government be able to provide? Keeping in mind, Nepal is a poor country and a good section of its people remains unemployed. 'May be the government will give people in the city around 15,000 to 20,000 thousand'; would that amount be enough to repair the house even? Perhaps not, in such a situation, how does Rahul convince people to leave their house or break it down? It is obvious people are going to resent him and the plans of the government. It is obvious that the people of Nepal are not going to see that what is being said is for their safety. The image of bringing down a building they call home is challenging their sense of security. The sense of house still standing represents hope and the idea of bringing that same house is equivalent to bringing down hope.

That is the problem of people in the city; the money that the Government of Nepal may provide is not going to be of any use. Yet, the people will take any amount given to them. Money is scarce now, and any amount given can be used for other purposes. The stories of rebuilding in the villages are slightly different. The government plans on giving them money to rebuild plus some other supports such as an aluminium sheet for a roof. Rahul points out to a man called Kunda on the other side of the road. Kunda is seated high on a heap of wood. A sum of 15,000 is not going to be enough even for these people. The houses in the city have cracks, whereas if you look at the houses situated here you will notice that ninety per cent of the houses have a wall that has fallen down. Here other than rebuilding, there is no option. 'There are many like Kunda in this part of the country, there is no way they can arrange to get that kind of money. There is no solution to the problems of rebuilding as of now. At least I do not see it, I go to all these houses and just do my job'.

Rahul has hit the nail on his head. There are so many practical problems when it comes to giving out monetary aid. How will the aid be given to the people in the village? They do not have bank accounts or any system in which money can be given to them transparently. Supplying food and money are two very different things; they sure cannot be done in the same manner. The problem of rebuilding is the biggest challenge for Nepal as of now! The monsoons are coming; there have been some really harsh thunderstorms that have hit the country. At times there have been hailstorms, finding shelter for Nepal is of utmost importance because failure to do so will result in huge number of deaths. This number I am afraid could be greater when compared to the number of lives lost in the earthquake itself.

In one of my opinion pieces published in *The Statesman* on 28 May 2015, I had said that the earthquake had provided Nepal with an opportunity to rebuild. This opportunity was not limited to the village or city, it is an opportunity that perhaps everybody in Nepal needed. When we consider the fact that Nepal as a country is built on a fault line, the number of quakes are going to continue for over a year. Perhaps they need the technology that helps in the making of Japanese cities, sure it is going to be expensive, and then again what is international aid for? If this technology cannot be used for people who deserve it and more importantly need it, how do we justify the large sums of money that is poured into research for creating such technology? Technology must be used for the betterment of human society after all and not for profit.

The streets of Kathmandu are congested, the buildings are too close to each other, and in a region such as this, it is dangerous. There must be a strong international will to help the people of Nepal. There are several ways in which Nepal requires the help of every world citizen. Nepal for me is a world that is so close to being pure. On the one hand, I am happy that the capitalistic world has stayed away, may be because the government has protected the country, but surely the government could use some help in rebuilding everything from the cracked walls of houses to a non-functional organisational system.

CHAPTER 16

Plastic

Many a times we come across posts about fun facts, these may include a certain fun fact about how much of time we normally waste on social media reading these weird stories. Well, not so long ago, before the Nepal Earthquake, I too was on a social networking site reading an article that seemed interesting. It was about how the materials we used in our everyday lives took to decompose, once placed under the Earth's surface. Since soil pollution had become such a big problem, I could not help but notice how much plastic is a contributing source.

Back in Bangalore, I had heard stories of certain drains that made us gag when we passed by, were once pristine lakes. They had served a picnic spots for generations, but my generation and the ones to come had traded their glory for an urbane existence. As I passed the slopes of the Himalayas, the many valleys and river gauges, I could not help but notice it bore a resemblance to the rivers that my teachers or parents had spoken of. To make matters worst, one day when I was making my way to the Buddhist centre at Boudha, Passang had told me a similar story. He was referring to drainage around Balaju Cholk, 'Once it was a river and my Grandfather would bring home fish from here'. I was shocked to see the kind of destruction that was taking place in this highly ecological, sensitive area. The drainage resembled the drains in Bangalore. A point I am sure won't be coming up in any tourist brochures.

As I went up the hills, I found plastic strewn in almost every area. It did not matter how remote the place was, plastic bags, throwaway sheets, and other such materials could be found. This was shocking to me as this was a region that was pure and beautiful. Interestingly, I noticed that every time relief had come to an area, it came along with plastic. As we are all aware, once it is put in the soil, plastic takes more than a hundred years to be decomposed.

What were we doing? While we went about solving one problem, we were giving rise to another problem. The lack of awareness and the dire need for material meant that people from the region were ignorant of the harmful effects of what was being given to them. While on the road,

I happened to discuss the matter with a young Tenzing Tsomo, an undergraduate student of the social works. I was talking to her simply because I came from a generation that was devoid of a chance to use the fruits of the earth. If there was any way in which I could protect a world I believed to be pure, I would. Tsomo seemed to agree that there was something wrong with the manner in which we went about doing things. Unfortunately, there is very little we could do, we realised we were using cloth bags to distribute rice, we took back every plastic sack we brought, but when it came to the packets of oil, we were helpless.

There were also the tarpaulin sheets that were being used by households as temporary shelter. Since the earthquake, the inflow of tarpaulin sheets into Nepal was high. The State of West Bengal had sent as many tarpaulin sheets as it could. After the first ten days, the whole of north India was short of Tarpaulin sheets. This is an indication of how much plastic has made its way into Nepal. As of now, there is no plan as to how this plastic will be treated once the need for its use ceases. While I do understand, if people say the first priority is to give people basic shelter and amenities, it cannot be at the cost of the environment. If you have felt the pain of the people, without any doubt you would not agree. Yet, I must ask the question? What is the use of all or discussions and education, when we are able to foresee a problem and yet make the same mistakes?

I very strongly believe the international organisations that are backed with some of the best minds, the greatest of experiences and resources must be able to organise relief work. Could there not have been an environmentally friendlier substance that could be used to provide shelter instead of tarpaulin sheets? At the moment, there is way too much of plastic that rests in the cradle of the Himalayan range. Perhaps it is too late to change the strategy; perhaps, it is too late to send something else other than tarpaulin sheets, but it would be foolish of the world community to not do anything about the amount of plastic that has already made its way into Nepal.

It may be too early to begin an operation to remove the plastic from Nepal at this moment. Yet, it is never too late to put in place a plan that will be easy to implement during natural disasters of this scale. If we had to put together a list of all the places in the world that deserve to be plastic-free, Nepal would definitely be one of the leading contenders to be on the top of that list. Yet, to expect them to make a decision and a conscious effort will be a folly. The truth is the country is too poor and it has had an overdose of suffering at the moment. This is why the international community will have to make a stand on its behalf.

The Himalayan region is way too important to be left alone. We must not forget that most of the water that flows into the rivers of the Indian sub-continent finds its sources in these regions. If the source is to be polluted, what use will it be to mount multi-billion dollar river cleansing schemes? No amount of cleaning will be able to quench the thirst of the millions.

Later, I noticed young Tsomo not change her mind about disposing a plastic bottle on the road. Instead, she ran into a nearby shop to use a dustbin. Perhaps now she realises that a greater number of lives depends on how her generation will take care of their environment. It is amazing how a casual chat can educate where reams of literature and hours spent on social media fail!

CHAPTER 17

The Earth Shook Again

I t had been like most days; except for there was an air
of optimism that filled the atmosphere around us. The
volunteers had travelled to a far-off location to deliver aid;
they had received a rousing welcome back at the Tibetan
centre. They were tired but refreshed as most believed they
had cheated death only to put a temporary smile on the
faces of people they had never met before. There were loads

of stories to be told, some terrifying, some sad, and some stories of joy. The experience when you make a difference in an unknown person's life can be life-changing! It was only eleven in the night, but that is a time that is considered very late in Kathmandu. Soon the lights of the Tibetan centre will go out, the group decides to call it a day. Passang is tired, yet happy as he announces a late morning for all the volunteers for their hard work had paid off.

The air of optimism continued as no tremor was felt during the night. There were some of us who could not get a sound sleep, because the earth was always moving in our head. But, there were some who did manage to get some good sleep. It was a pleasant morning in Kathmandu, not surprising as there was a hailstorm the previous night, hours before the relief truck made its way to the Tibetan centre. There were little children playing everywhere, Tingmos, a form of Tibetan bread was served for breakfast. Slowly the volunteers began to make their presence at the Tibetan centre. Soon the elders would begin prayers for the safe return of volunteers belonging to the RTYC.

Passang and his core team were getting ready to begin their meetings; there were important matters to be discussed, funding and the next operation high on the agenda. The others in the group had time to spare and so they began catching up on the things they had missed while they were away in Jiri. I too had time to spare but I had work to do, my blog entry had to be made, and I was eager to do that. I settled down to type out my views and experiences, everything felt good, and I do not know how time flew. The blog post was ready, my lap top, power bank, and mobile phone was charged. I was all set for the next relief operation. At this point, my lap top began to act strange and for some reason it would not let me upload my post, it would not shut down it, would not do anything that I wanted it to do. I left all my belongings in the place that I used to sleep and went out to put my stuff in order. It was now close to one in the afternoon and that meant it was time for me to go and help with the packing of relief material.

All of a sudden, I heard the gate slam, there was the feeling of the ground I was standing on dropped itself to a lower level. I rushed out; this was the biggest of earthquakes that I had felt. As I made it out, there were people scrambling to the open areas screaming. There was panic everywhere and it almost seemed like a stampede had broken out at the Tibetan centre. There was nowhere to run as the roads around the centre are narrow and the electric wires hanging over the polls were a threat to life. The Tibetan volunteers swung into action, it seemed like they were almost fighting with their elders, but they were trying to get everybody to calm down. There were a few small injuries that were reported.

The ground continued to move as panic began to take hold of the entire city of Kathmandu. I could feel it move myself. It can be best described as the feeling one gets when he spins herself or himself round and round several times before coming to a stop. It is the same feeling; standing up straight is a challenge. However, sitting down is not an option because you may get stamped by people who are frantically running to find safety. As soon as the earth found stability, there was traffic jam everywhere. The people around me had got a grip by now; I realised that all my important materials were stuck under the basement. It was too risky to go down, yet it had to be done. Once I had collected what I needed, I decided I had a chance to report from the ground. I got to the main roads of Boudha Gate. Every now and then there was the passing of an ambulance. The shutters were down, and the army had arrived to take stock of the situation. Just then the ground moved again! This time it was an aftershock measuring 3.0 on the Richter scale. Buildings had collapsed; there were some leaning on other buildings.

The whole of Kathmandu began to empty their houses. The shops that were selling foams and plastic sheets found themselves in business, yet most of them chose to remain close. There was also the sight of families that had cars leaving the city with their bags packed and loaded over the roof of the car. People were beginning to flee the city. The taxi drivers stayed on the road not for the business but as a service to the people. They did not demand to be paid a fare, if a person wanted to give them an amount, they accepted whatever was given to them. They carried the maximum number of people they could as the traffic situation got from bad to worse.

The local people of Nepal were showing some great resolve at this point. When a building falls, at times there are people inside who need to be rescued. The protocol says people must wait for the army to come in, not that the army took long to come. The reaction of the army was as quick, but even then it takes a few minutes before the army can reach a spot and organise itself. Those few minutes are very crucial. The longer it takes, the more difficult it becomes for a person to be taken out of the rubble. Normal citizens of Nepal were responsible for pulling out a good number of their friends from buildings that were collapsing. As Kathmandu continued to shut down, the earth stopped shaking. The earthquake had hit the eastern side of Kathmandu, the heart of most relief operations. The eastern side of Kathmandu had not witnessed the strength of the first earth quake; the second one had come for it. Ninety per cent of the houses in the eastern side are damaged. People were fleeing the city now, which was not surprising as Kathmandu is the city of migrants. Every person was trying to get onto a bus that could take him home.

The mobile phone networks were also jammed, and communication had become close to not possible. There were calls that were being made by people of Nepal desperately trying to see if their loved ones were safe. Life had just gotten worse for relief volunteers like me who were from a different country as it had become impossible to get in touch with our loved ones from across the border. I had seen my share of despair. I was able to get in touch with Passang, who had gone to check on the well-being of his family. I had to now make it back to the Tibetan centre.

Once I had got back, the Tibetan settlement had settled down well, there were a few broken bits of buildings that were on the road. When I met Passang, he informed me about the death of people on the parallel road. The Government of Nepal had managed to save a lot of people's lives by evacuating people whose houses were colour-coded red. Yet, there were people who had died; interestingly, this was not because they were inside the buildings that had collapsed. They had died because the buildings had fallen on the roads where they were stranded. This was the biggest factor influencing the loss of life.

It was time for me to leave Nepal, I had realised this as I watched Passang's family move to the streets. It was not right for me to ask him to let me stay with him. I gave him a couple of Tarpaulin sheets, I had ordered from India, he gave me his tent to get through the night. As I made my way away from the Tibetan settlement, I looked back one last time to find a community that I had grown very fond of. Did I want to leave, of course not! But, I had to leave. The 7.4 was not an earthquake it was more of an aftershock. It did not break too many houses or claim too many lives, it had claimed hope. As I tried to leave Nepal, I found it increasingly hard to do so, the airport closed down for forty-eight hours and people were scrambling to get out. I ran into several foreign nationals, who had come to help with relief work. All of them had decided to leave; as I continued to feel bad about leaving Nepal in this hour of need, I met a girl young Caroline, who like me had no will of leaving Kathmandu. I joined her in distributing biscuits and things alike to the people on the streets of Nepal. As we ran out of materials to distribute, we decided we needed to get some more, as we dragged ourselves from shop to shop, we found that the rates had soared. Caroline said to me it was time to leave, the both of us did leave Kathmandu that night. We had found the strength to leave Nepal because we had realised the hope we carried for the people of Nepal had burned out.

Tom Bodett once said, 'They say a person needs just three things to be truly happy in this world: someone to love, something to do, and something to hope for'. The people of Nepal had lost some of all three things after the 7.4 aftershock. I had lost hope, with the prices skyrocketing, I was now a burden to the people of Nepal. There were a few choices I could make at the time, I decided to leave Nepal. How can you end a book with the last message being 'there is no hope', you would think. I would like to keep it like that, because all of us do feel hopeless at times. It is human to do so, as time passes, hope will rekindle strength. I could not wait for my strength to come back, I hope you do!

A few weeks after I reached Bangalore, I kept myself updated with the happenings in Nepal. I found that the Tibetan youth had resumed rescue efforts. The places they were going to were challenging, and my heart longed to be with them. I pray for the people of Nepal now, I know God may not keep them safe. However, I do know God will inspire people to reach out to them in times of need.